Transitioning Your Aging Parent

Transitioning Your Aging Parent
A 5 Step Guide Through Crisis & Change

Dale C. Carter

ISBN: 978-0-557-44740-4

Advance Praise for
Transitioning Your Aging Parent: A 5 Step Guide Through Crisis & Change

I t's almost as though you took all my years of training and managed to put order to it. The ADAPT method of caregiving will decrease stress and give great comfort to families in the eldercare world. My fear is that we can't get it out to people fast enough.

> ~ P.K. Beville, M.S.
> Founder, Second Wind Dreams & Geriatric Specialists
> Author, *Virtual Dementia Tour Series*

This deceptively small book is one that every adult with a parent should read. It skillfully guides you step by step through the process of helping your parent's transition. It's full of helpful resources for you and your parent. It will be a lifesaver in a time of crisis, but I recommend you don't wait until then. Get the book now and follow Dale Carter's ADAPT method to prepare you and your parent for the inevitable changes ahead.

> ~ Debra Joy, CEO, Bcelebrated

For those entering the unchartered waters as a caregiver, *Transitioning Your Aging Parent: A 5 Step Guide Through Crisis & Change* is an invaluable life raft. Dale Carter provides readers with a framework to help create solutions for the most complex family challenges. The book outlines countless resources and creative ideas to help the most frazzled caregiver reduce guilt and offer the freedom to help spend more quality time with their loved ones.

~ Steve Gurney, Publisher,
Guide to Retirement Living SourceBook

Whether you are a business professional trying to help your aging parents, a long distance caregiver or a stay-at-home caregiver, you need *Transitioning Your Aging Parent: A 5 Step Guide Through Crisis & Change*. Dale's ADAPT Method provides a step-by-step plan which changes overwhelming situations into manageable ones. My favorite part of the ADAPT Method is that it balances respecting our aging parent while understanding the needs of the caregiver. Thank you Dale for creating a straightforward, quick-to-read guidebook for helping our parents transition through the aging process.

~ Viki Kind, MA
Author, *The Caregiver's Path to Compassionate Decision Making –*
Making Choices for Those Who Can't

Dedication and Acknowledgments

I dedicate this book to my mother, Beverly Jean,
for facing crisis and change with courage and a positive attitude,

and to my husband Bill, and my children, David, Christopher and
Rachel,
for their support and encouragement.

~~~

My special thanks to all the colleagues and friends who read my
manuscript,
ensuring its completeness and accuracy.
Thank you for your dedication, compassion, and advocacy on
behalf of our elderly.

Thanks to:
P.K. Beville, Denise Brown, Catherine Burch, Robbie Deike,
Patricia Druley, Val Eigner, Steve Gurney, Debra Joy, Viki Kind,
Lisa Rogers Lee, Mary Morgan, Barb Roberts, Lisa Sneddon,
Brenda Torres,
and Amy Magan (University of Indianapolis Center for Aging &
Community)

~~~

Please visit www.TransitionAgingParents.com for information
and insight
to help your parent *thrive and find joy in every stage of life.*

Contents

Introduction

Why Write This?

How can we help our aging parents navigate the many changes they will face over time? These changes may include one or more of the following:

- having home modifications done to facilitate "aging in place"
- giving up driving
- selling their home
- moving in with a family member or to a senior care facility

As a loving son or daughter, we want to help our parent while respecting their wishes. Wouldn't it be wonderful to do that in a way that minimizes conflict and brings our whole family closer together? Through my personal experience, I discovered a way. It's not without hard work and patience, but I will show you how to help your aging parent transition. By definition, *transition* is an event that results in transformation. What a lovely image. With each change that we guide our parent through, we are helping him or her transform!

Let me share my story. I am an adult daughter of an elderly mother (the most common dynamic in caregiving in the United States today.)1 In March 2008, my husband and I were enjoying life as empty nesters, and I was working as a project management consultant. One day I got a call that my mother had an apparent stroke and had been rushed to the hospital. At that point in time I had no knowledge about aging issues, geriatric healthcare, or senior living options. I was living six hundred miles away from my mother, with my only brother on vacation and unreachable.

Today, my mother is healthier and happier than any of us can recall. When I reflect on how I got my mother through her crisis, helped her transition, and prepared for *our* future, I realized it was my professional training and experience as an educator and project manager that enabled me to deal with the crisis at hand, as well as prepare for her future. It reminds me of the pilot who landed the plane on the Hudson River in December 2008. He said it was his professional training and years of experience that enabled him to know exactly what to do and to perfectly execute the landing.

I realize not everyone facing the aging of a parent has the training and experience I have. I decided to write this book to share the steps I used to help transition my mother through her health and living crisis. Regardless of the type of transition your parent is facing, you can utilize the framework I am about to share with you. This book does not offer information about any particular aging problem. There are excellent information sites out there that I will reference for that kind of information. Instead, this book will show you how to approach any problem your aging parent is facing in a structured, but caring, manner.

When you have an aging parent, you don't want to have to be making decisions on the fly. You want—and yes, need—a plan. This book will not waste your time. It will provide a structured approach for the next time you need to transition your parent. It will help you find ways to prevent or deal with problems and challenges along the way. It will allow you to focus on being present with your aging parent, the rest of your family, and yourself!

A Personal Story

Back to March 2008. I was in the kitchen of my home in Indiana when I received a call from my mother's friend in Maryland that Mom was being hospitalized with what was thought to be a stroke. Mom had been homebound for the three months prior to the incident. Her physical health, emotional state, and the state of her home had deteriorated rapidly during that time. While my brother visited each weekend and assured me things were fine, they were not. I had begun searching for area services for her such as Meals on Wheels, a home health aide, and a cleaning service. But my mother declined all offers, and continued to say she was fine. Finally, her health declined to the point of crisis.

While I would not wish this crisis on any person or any family, it was a wake-up call for both my mother and me. Even as I was preparing to drive to my mother's home, I began to carve out a plan in my mind and prioritize the things I would have to tackle. I had no time to search the Internet or find the right book. I identified and sought out the resources I thought I would need, created a rough plan on my own, made preliminary calls, and drove back to Maryland. I didn't know if my mother had weeks, months, or years to live.

When I arrived, I realized I had never seen her in such a weak, ill state, and I was appalled to see the state of her home. It wasn't just cluttered—it was filthy. No bed or chair was empty, pills were ground into rugs, paperwork was piled and scattered everywhere, and the kitchen sink was full of crusted pots. The cleaning service I hired declared the house should be condemned.

It should have been overwhelming, but I recall sitting on a stair step and clearly thinking, "No one should ever live like this." At that moment, I decided I would do whatever it would take to provide my mother with the best quality of life for as long as she had left. That desire, that image of the end goal, is what would sustain me for the hard weeks that followed.

The good news is Mom did not have a stroke. In a three-month period and over the course of two more visits, I was able to get her health stabilized and her home totally renovated and sold. I also helped Mom to find the retirement community of her dreams.

Certainly your parent and your relationship with your parent will be different from mine. The transition you are facing or will face in the future will also likely be different. But through the work I've done at TransitionAgingParents.com and by talking with adult children all over the country, I came to realize there is an urgent need for people to have a simple, clear guide for facing transitions with their parents.

It is my sincere hope that my framework for transition and what I share will help you better prepare for the future with your aging parent, and also to respond more effectively when confronted by a crisis. Whether the challenge is physical health, mental health, housing, financial, or legal, I believe this guide will help you understand the situation, come to the right decision, and be able to take the right action.

Who Will Benefit from This Guide?

Whether you are an adult child, a family member, or a professional caregiver, this guide is written for you. If you are in the midst of crisis, you can immediately put my suggested framework into practice. If you sense your parent deteriorating, you can incorporate this framework into your thinking and approach. If you are a family member, you can share this with your entire family to facilitate the conversation that's needed. If you're a caregiver, you can share this with the families you are serving. They will be most grateful to be empowered.

What is really important is that you are willing to:

- Commit to listening to and helping your parent pursue a good quality of life.
- Listen to and communicate with siblings, family members, and experts.
- Plan carefully, but be flexible as circumstances change.

What Will This Guide Not Provide?

This guide is not a cookbook solution or quick fix for problems with your aging parent. Even though the process I outline appears clear and straightforward, each step involves a lot of hard work. If you are unable to invest the time and patience into planning and the transition process, then this process is not for you.

What Will You Learn?

You will learn how to approach any change or transition in your parent's life with clarity and with confidence. You will learn:

1. How to "actively" listen to your parent and clearly understand your parent's situation.
2. How to measure your own capacity.
3. How to know who to involve in decision making.
4. How to reach consensus.
5. How to create a plan for transition.
6. How to find experts and resources that will help your plan succeed.
7. How to carry out the plan and help your parent adjust to the changes.

What if You Have Two Aging Parents?

In writing this guide, I assume you only have one aging parent. Before we move forward, I want address the issue of two aging parents in this short section.

1. *If you have one parent who is ill and one parent who is relatively healthy,* be careful to pay special attention to the healthy parent. (Let's assume the healthy spouse is a male, to keep the language simple.) He will be in the role of primary caregiver and needs all the physical and emotional support possible. Work with him to create a list of what needs to be done and see what you can do or arrange to have done. You will probably need to make this a slow transition, gradually taking over tasks, one at a time, and guiding him to outside help. Listen closely to understand his fears and needs. Make sure he takes care of his own health and gets respite.

2. *If both of your parents are ill and need care,* then you will want to go through the ASSESS phase for each one, as each of their needs may be different. Also be mindful and respectful of their relationship and needs as a couple in all decisions being made.

What if You Are an Only Child?

In writing this guide, I assume there are two or more siblings. Before we move forward, I want to address the issue of the only child as a caregiver. Many of us may think that an only child is fortunate to not have to deal with the different perspectives and needs of siblings. But the only child has no sibling to share concerns with or to share in the caregiving. That situation can quickly lead to isolation and being overwhelmed. My suggestion is to build deep relationships with close friends who will be there for you, much as siblings would. Be sure to also seek professional help, support groups, and respite.

Terminology

For the rest of the book, I have chosen to use the terms *she* and *daughter* to denote any adult child of an aging parent, female or male.

(Tip: If you are a male caregiver, be sure to read this excellent AARP article that addresses the approaches and concerns unique to the male caregiver:

http://bulletin.aarp.org/yourhealth/caregiving/articles/the_new _face_of_caregiving.html)

Chapter 1

The ADAPT® Method

Here is my framework, plain and simple. I created the acronym ADAPT® to make the steps easy to remember. *Adapt* is what the whole transition is all about. A major change in anyone's life requires adapting. But transitioning an aging parent requires adaptation by you, your parent, and the entire family. You all need to be active participants in this process.

The ADAPT®Method

Assess—> Discuss—> As a family—> Plan—> Transition

A is for Assess

D is for Discuss

A is for "As a family"

P is for Plan

T is for Transition

Assess

In the Assess phase, you will *observe, listen,* and *have important conversations with your parent.* Let go of past baggage. Let go of wishing that things were as they used to be. If you never had a good relationship with your parent, you may be dreading this. But from my own personal experience, I know this is an opportunity for a new start.

To have those critical conversations, you'll want to use open-ended questions. At this stage, you are not suggesting anything. You are simply asking your parent about their personal wishes so you can understand their perspective. You need to build a foundation of understanding before you can discern what the real issue is, before you can consider options and needed changes. Here are a couple of the open-ended questions I used to open up dialogue with my mother:

- "What if you can't go back to driving (due to your medications)? What kind of services do you think you will need?"
- "After your friend Jean's hip replacement, she decided to move in with her son. If you were Jean, what would your preferences be?"

At the end of this process, you will be able to say, "I understand my parent's situation and perspective, at this point in time."

Another key component of the Assess phase is to assess yourself and your situation. You will need to consider your own health needs and work and family responsibilities, as well as your support network. This is a critical step that far too many adult children fail to consider.

Discuss

In the Discuss phase, you will learn about your parent's wishes. With the help of family members, you'll consider the possible solutions to your parent's challenges. Afterwards, you'll be able to confidently say to your parent, "Given what I learned from listening to you, I believe these are some viable options to consider, moving forward." Your parent needs time to mentally transition. They will likely struggle to imagine what life will be like after this change.

As a family

Everyone needs to be involved. Not just you and your aging parent. You should include your aging parent's spouse, your parent's siblings, and your siblings. They should all be informed and asked to offer input. This may sound like opening up a can of worms, but there is so much value in getting everyone's ideas and buy-in. It is so important to get everyone involved now so they feel they have been a part of the planning and that their concerns and needs have been acknowledged. Stephen Covey in his book, *7 Habits of Highly Effective_People,* talks about the emotional bank account in which we make deposits to or withdrawals from family relationships. This is the time when you need to be making deposits. Build up those emotional bank accounts and the foundation of trust now. Later, when you get into the hard work of making decisions, dividing up tasks, helping a parent make a challenging transition, there will be plenty of withdrawals. Invest the time and energy now to build a strong foundation of common understanding and family trust.

Plan

All of us have likely been involved in planning a project, work-related or personal. Maybe it was renovating a home, selling a house and moving, sending a child off to college, or planning a wedding. Did you realize the planning portion of a project consumes up to 60 percent of the total project time? If your project was successful, you know the tedious, time-consuming nature of planning. You probably also know what happens if you don't plan. When it comes to helping your parent transition, you do not want to wing it. Your aging parent's health, safety, and quality of life are at stake. You need to do your best to get it right.

During one or more family meetings, you'll engage in a process of shared decision making to reach agreement about direction and next steps. Don't worry. I'll provide suggestions on how best to facilitate and conduct your meeting. I'll provide a list of resources, and a template for a detailed plan. You need to walk away from the family meeting knowing who needs to do what, when it needs to happen, and to understand why and how the various steps will occur.

Transition

This Transition phase is where the rubber meets the road. This is the point at which all the observing, listening, striving to understand, research, negotiation, planning, and buy-in pays off. If you follow my framework, you and your family will be positioned well to help your aging parent with any transition.

Also keep one very important point in mind as you navigate through the transition. Even though you've done everything right and covered every base, it is very likely that your parent or a sibling may—right before the change is to take place—suddenly change their mind, get emotional, or lash out at whoever is closest. This is not unusual, and should be expected. Most transitions are large, life-changing experiences. And as much as you are abiding by your parent's wishes, they will feel emotions of loss, anxiety, sadness, and fear. Set your expectations accordingly, and by all means, be flexible, patient, and understanding as you *stay the course.*

How Does It All Fit Together?

By now, you probably realize this framework is a sequential process. For every transition you are helping your parent through, you must follow each step in order.

What if you skip a step in the process to save time or because you're uncomfortable with family dynamics (or for some other reason)?

If you skip Assess, you will not have a true understanding of your parent, their wishes, or the starting point. If you have read Stephen Covey's book, *7 Habits of_Highly Effective People*, you'll recall Habit 5 was "Seek First to Understand and to Be Understood." Never is that more true than when we are trying to help our parents. I can pretty much guarantee if you go in with a "know it all" mentality, you and your parent will end up frustrated and discouraged. You will not be helping your parent.

If you skip the next two steps, Discuss and As a Family, you will likely face lack of support and continuing interpersonal conflicts within your family. You do not want to be the one left to do all the work. That can be exhausting, expensive, and incredibly stressful. I heard someone describe caregiving as a marathon, not a sprint. None of us can see into the future to know what challenges are ahead. You and your parent will need the strength, support, and love of your whole family as your parent moves along the continuum of aging. This may well be the hardest step of all. To have the family come together and reach a consensus means dropping the old sibling rivalries and perceived family roles. This is incredibly tough the first time, especially in a time of crisis. But remember why you are doing this. As Covey says in his Habit 2, *"Begin with the End in Mind."* You may wish to come up with a vision and mission statement. For my mother, we all decided we wanted her to have "quality of life for as long as she lived."

If you skip the next step, Planning, you'll likely face time lost, money lost, an unhappy or unsafe parent, and/or a split in the family. You must lay out a timeline, with all the tasks and responsibilities. If you make a choice that seems risky, have a contingency plan in mind. If this all sounds like something you've used in your work—project management—it is. There is too much at stake here to skip the planning step.

The Transition is where all the hard work and preparation pays off. This is the "Action" phase when the agreed-upon change takes place for your parent. Follow your plan, noting problems and making adjustments.

So, let's get on with it, the detail behind my *ADAPT*® framework.

The ADAPT®Method

Assess—> Discuss—> As a family—> Plan—> Transition

A is for Assess

D is for Discuss

A is for "As a family"

P is for Plan

T is for Transition

Chapter 2

Assess: *Drop the Assumptions. Listen and Learn*

Your Parent

H ow can you best assess your parent's situation? Start with a genuine desire to understand your parent. Put yourself in their shoes. We've all heard how important it is to be in the present moment. Put other distractions (mental or physical) aside. Put your total focus on your parent.

(Tip: I purchased a hardbound notebook that I used to capture all my observations, contact information, notes, and to-do tasks. I strongly suggest you do the same. Keep it with you and use it! I referred to it constantly.)

Observe. Become a detached observer. In marketing they call it ethnography. Put all your assumptions and beliefs aside. And just observe. Spend a day (or more) with your parent and walk beside them. Be supportive, but quiet. You want to get to know your parent in their current state. Watch how they move, who they talk with, and what they have trouble with. Even if they live close by and you see them often, this *detached observation* will give you accurate, verified information. Here are some key things to observe:

- Can your parent get through daily activities (bathing, dressing, toileting, cooking) okay?
- Is your parent's house reasonably clean? Is paperwork organized and bills paid?
- Can she get to the grocery store and prepare healthy meals? Be sure to peek in the refrigerator and check expiration dates.
- Is she still driving? If so, ride with her. Observe her driving and the condition of the car.
- Does she fall or feel unsteady? Are there tripping hazards?
- Is she strong enough to get in and out of bed or her favorite chair by herself?
- How much social interaction is she getting?

Listen. Listen empathetically as your parent speaks. I found that I had to quiet myself so I could listen without all too quickly responding. Listen to tone of voice and watch body language. You can learn so much. I used to get annoyed with my mother because she would repeat the same negative comments over and over again, how a friend was always dressed beautifully, lived in an expensive villa, or had taken a vacation she could never afford. A common remark was, "I could tell she (the friend) felt she was better than anyone else." One day, instead of turning a deaf ear, I tried to understand the underlying meaning. I suddenly realized a theme that permeated my mother's life was a sense of low self-esteem. I finally understood the reason behind her shopaholic tendencies.

By observing and listening, you gain awareness of your parent's life and concerns. You gain their trust. You're not viewed as an adversary; you become a partner in their journey. When you and your parent recognize this, it is a true turning point. I recall the exact moment I felt this. In the midst of my mother's crisis, I understood that not only did I need to help her, but I had to do it in a way that preserved her dignity and empowered her. I cannot tell you how much my own understanding changed when I realized that. At that moment, I could feel myself letting go of past perceptions and personal baggage, and turning my focus to the future. You may not experience such an epiphany, but you will likely experience a real shift in your perspective.

Engage in critical conversations. Despite the specific transition at hand, it's important to have a number of critical conversations (outlined below) as early as possible. These conversations add to your foundation of understanding, and include health, home environment and safety, social support, mental and emotional states, and financial and legal situations.

Despite the potential transition issue, you need to have an understanding of all these areas. Any change in one area can impact the other areas. It's like a machine with many moving parts.

Health. Ask your parent about their primary care physicians and other specialists. It's important to know if she trusts her doctors.

Ask about any illness and prognosis. Sit with your parent, and look at the bottles of all her medications, dosages and warnings on the labels.

(Tip: For a comprehensive review of all of your parent's medications, check with her Medicare Prescription Drug Plan or pharmacist to see if "Medication Therapy Management" service is available. To understand how a typical service works, here is a description of the offering by SilverScript: http://www .silverscript.com/en-US/medication-therapy-management-programs.aspx)

Also, ask what method your parent uses to stay on her medication schedule.

(Tip: Check out technologies being offered for medication reminders and dispensers. Laurie Orlov does a great job of

reviewing the various products, along with their pros and cons, at http://www.gilbertguide.com/articles/aging-in-place -technology-medication-reminders/)

It's also a good idea to create a list of medications and dosages. Post a copy on your parent's refrigerator (in case of emergency) and keep a copy for yourself. Ask if she's having any particular health-related problems. My mother could not get her diabetes monitor to work, so for months she had not taken her blood sugar reading daily, as she should have. I helped her read the directions and start using the monitor. Simple things like this often do not get shared unless we ask. You might offer to go to the doctor with your parent for your parent's next appointment.

As you have probably already experienced, an elderly person's health can change very quickly. The reality of multiple, chronic conditions, multiple medications, and the aging process is that change is always imminent.

<u>Cognitive and emotional state.</u> Your parent may not consider a lapse in memory a health problem. Many people and families rationalize subtle changes away. But it is important to detect signs of dementia or depression and report them to your parent's primary care physician. In a disease such as Alzheimer's, the earlier a diagnosis is made, the more effective the medications are in delaying the disease.

Here is a short list of symptoms of dementia:

- Having difficulty recalling recent events.
- Not recognizing familiar people and places.
- Having trouble finding the right words to express thoughts or name objects.
- Having difficulty performing calculations.
- Having problems planning and carrying out tasks, such as balancing a checkbook, following a recipe, or writing a letter.
- Having trouble exercising judgment, such as knowing what to do in an emergency.

- Having difficulty controlling moods or behaviors. Depression is common, and agitation or aggression may occur.
- Not keeping up personal care, such as grooming or bathing.

Here is a short list of symptoms of depression:

- Loss of interest in things they have enjoyed in the past.
- Thinking and speaking more slowly than normal.
- Having trouble concentrating, remembering, and making decisions.
- Having changes in their eating and sleeping habits.
- Being preoccupied with death and/or suicide.
- Having feelings of guilt, worthlessness, or hopelessness.

Know that a person may have a combination of both dementia and depression, especially in the beginning stages of cognitive decline. Twenty to 40 percent of people with dementia also suffer from depression.[2] It is most helpful and also important to keep a log of specific observations to share with your parent's physician, as well as with other family members.

(Tip: For a more thorough discussion of dementia and depression, the Alzheimer's Foundation offers an excellent article at: http://www.alzfdn.org/AboutDementia/depression .html)

Home environment and safety. Toronto gerontologist and recognized expert on seniors' mobility, Dr. James Watzke, shared that both his elderly parents died in a house fire three years ago.[3] Ensuring our parent's safety is a challenge, even for the experts.

The bathroom and kitchen are the areas that need the most scrutiny. AARP offers an excellent interactive home safety checklist. You may want to utilize this in your assessment process: http://assets.aarp.org/external_sites/caregiving/checklists /checklist_homeSafety.html

Ask if your parent has experienced dizziness or tripping. My mother shared that she was anxious about going down the steps to the basement to do her laundry, concerned she would fall and no one would find her. It was not an unfounded concern. One out of every three Americans age sixty-five or more has a pretty serious fall at least once a year.[4]

That conversation led us to getting her a Life Alert personal emergency response system (PERS).

(Tip: Check out the exciting new technology in PERS. Wellcore offers an Emergency Response system with automatic fall detection. http://wellcore.com/)

Social support. Does your parent get enough social interaction with friends, neighbors, and in the community? How often does she get human interaction and with whom? Does she interact with neighbors? Can she get to church regularly, if she chooses?

Does your parent know who to turn to for help with home maintenance and problems with crime? My mother had trouble with local teens vandalizing the exterior of her home. It was both a nuisance and a source of anxiety for her.

Does your parent have access to the Internet? Would she be interested in learning? There are excellent new software and hardware solutions being designed specifically for the elderly. In the Bonus section at the end of this book, I share the link to one such software provider, Famililink. It is software that I have thoroughly tested and taught my mother to use.

Financial and legal affairs. Ask if your parent has a tax accountant, attorney, or other financial or legal consultants. Don't be surprised to find a patchwork of services—or none at all.

The important thing is that you gain an understanding of your parent's financial situation (both short-term and long-term), and that all key legal documents are in one place, and you know where that place is.

If your parent has not completed the key documents or they are scattered, take time to gather these and review them together.

Doing such a review in non-crisis mode is one of the best things you can do for your parent and yourself.

The documents you gather should include:

- Bank accounts
- Insurance companies
- Deed and titles
- Loan information
- Social Security and Medicare numbers.
- Military history, affiliations, and papers
- Up-to-date, notarized will, kept in a safe place
- Living Will or other Advanced Directive (meeting current state law)
- Durable Power of Attorney.
- Instructions for funeral services and burial

(Tip: If documents are stored in a safety deposit box, make sure your name is on the box, too.)

When my mother was in crisis, I didn't have time to locate all the important papers as I was making a rough financial estimate of her assets and income. An interim shortcut I took was to review each of her 1099s (from recent income tax preparation). My mother and I called every financial institution listed in her 1099s. I obtained the type of account, the disbursement method and frequency, and the amount remaining in the account. I also requested that all disbursements be sent "direct deposit" to my mother's bank account.

Family Members

The next step is to talk with each family member who needs to be involved in future decisions and care for your parent. This includes your parent's spouse, parent's siblings or pseudo-siblings (best friend), and your siblings. (We'll wait to discuss your immediate family, spouse and children, in the next step.)

You will need to have a similar conversation with each of these people. Often, due to distance or family rifts, we've not stayed in touch with some of our relatives, perhaps our siblings. Now is the time to put the past behind and think about how you can best help your parent. Start the conversation by showing interest in your family member's life. Have an open-ended conversation.

(Tip: Choosing the right location for a conversation can often make all the difference. Consider taking a walk in the outdoors or meeting in a quiet coffee shop. These conversations can be overwhelming, but hang in there.)

After you've listened to your family member, share that you've spent time with your parent and what you've observed and learned. It may be helpful to share a one-page summary of your observations (including what areas you perceive to be high-risk and high-priority). Explain that you're talking with each family member and are continuing to gather all the needed information and their insight in preparation for a family meeting.

Don't be surprised if the person gets defensive. A sibling may say they see things differently and try to push old hot buttons. Stay on point. State that you still have to gather information from your parent's doctors, neighbors, friends, and church. And that you'll be scheduling a family meeting soon.

Know that you have planted the seed. Your sibling will likely need time for all this information to sink in. This step will make the family meeting much less contentious.

Parent's Physicians

If your parent has given her permission (to her physicians), you can reach out to them and share about your mother's health conditions. If she will not grant you permission, you can still send a letter to the doctor, explaining your concerns. The primary care physician (PCP) is definitely the key person to reach out to.

Too many families suffer in silence as health and home conditions deteriorate.

When my mother had her health crisis and was hospitalized, one of the first calls I made was to my mother's specialist at Johns Hopkins who was treating her for an auto-immune disease. I realized the hospital probably had not notified him. He immediately contacted her PCP to coordinate her care.

I still have to remind my mother to get referrals to specialists through her PCP office so that care will be coordinated. My mother often went to specialists on her own who ended up treating her symptoms—but not the root cause—while she continued to deteriorate.

Finally, realize that your PCP can make referrals to any services you may need. When I told the PCP about my mother's need for help in her home, he referred me to the local Visiting Angels. I later learned PCPs also make recommendations for geriatric care managers.

Parent's Neighbors and Friends

Check in with your parent's neighbors and friends. Make sure you have their contact information and they have yours. My mother's best friend was a wonderful resource for me. Unfortunately, my mother had never shared her friend's full name and phone number with me, nor did her friend have mine. Her friend had to demand it from my mother as my mother was placed in an ambulance. The friend became a lifeline for me. She shared her perspective of my mother's challenges, her social network, and wishes my mother had shared with her. She was also a lady of great strength and calm.

Your parent's neighbors have likely changed over the years. Ideally, your parent should have at least one neighbor who serves as your "eyes and ears" when you are not there. It should be someone who knows what's going on in the neighborhood, who keeps an eye out for her, perhaps sees her daily at the mailbox or in the driveway. Again, be sure you have that person's contact info and they have yours.

Parent's Place of Worship

Your parent's place of worship is another great resource. Again, share your name and contact info. Be sure to ask about support programs, such as Stephens Ministry or elderly visitation programs. The church or synagogue can also provide names of members who can help you with community resources. It was through a church member that I found out about my mother's Area Agency on Aging, Meals on Wheels, a free walker, and transportation across town to specialists' appointments. Of course, you will want to notify the church/synagogue office of any change in your parent's health or situation so they will know to reach out and support you and your parent.

Stop! Time for a Sanity Check.

I have just covered lots of information. Take a step back. Make a list of all the people you need to speak with. What will you share with them? What will you ask them? A conversation is always easier if you've listed out some guiding questions and know what you hope or need to achieve. The first time having such dialogue is definitely the hardest.

There is something called the 40-70 rule.[5] If you're aged 40 and your parents are aged 70, you should be having these conversations now. If you're not in crisis, you have time to pace yourself—just don't procrastinate. If you're in crisis right now, don't blame yourself or feel guilty for waiting. Just work through the steps as quickly and thoughtfully as possible.

Chapter 3

Assess: *Know Thyself*

C ertainly adult children need to be empathetic and responsive to an aging parent. But that does not mean you disregard yourself, your personal life, and your responsibilities.

There is the realization that this is your only mother (father). They have always been there for you, and now you want to be there for them. After all, you don't know how much longer they will be with you. And you literally jump in, head first, and totally dedicate yourself and say, "Whatever it takes, I'll do it." I know. I had this exact reaction when my mother had her crisis.

But stop first before you leap into it. You have no way of knowing how many years and how much care/assistance your parents will need. You cannot see into the future and predict what health conditions may arise. If a person lives to be sixty-five, their average life expectancy is another eighteen years!6 The average number of chronic health conditions for those over age sixty-five is three. The prevalence of Alzheimer's disease doubles every five years beyond age sixty-five.7 Based on those statistics, most of us will be caring for one or more parents for many years through all sorts of transitions and challenges.

We have to understand our own capacity and limitations. And we will have to continue to evaluate those over time. Assessing your own capacity will allow you to set boundaries and limits without guilt. You will feel justified in reaching out to family and friends for help. You'll avoid that feeling of being so overwhelmed that you don't even know what to ask for, how to ask for it, or who to ask. We all know what happens then. You shut yourself off from others, hunker down, and spiral out of control.

Your Personal Health and Capacity

Consider your own personal health. Do you have any serious or chronic health conditions? Do you have the recommended regular physical, dental, eye exams, and screenings? Caregivers are at risk for depression and a shortened lifespan. That is because caregivers frequently disregard their own health. Just because you feel healthy now, don't think your body can endure years of uninterrupted stress.

What is your energy level? Some people thrive on crisis situations and deadlines. I worked for such a gentleman. Know that you cannot sustain that level of adrenaline and response for long. As I said earlier, caregiving is a marathon, not a sprint. Making sure you get on a proper sleep schedule is so important. In our multi-tasking, online world, we never seem to have *enough hours in the day. I love Stephen Covey's advice to drop the "Not Urgent, Not Important: junk mail, busywork, trivia, "escape" activities,* and focus instead on the *Not Urgent, but Important: preparation, problem prevention, planning, relationship building, values clarification, true recreation ("re-creation")."* Identify and work on changing any deep-seated poor habits.

Work Responsibilities

Work is a huge part of our lives. Many of us are working longer hours than ever before and are required to be more and more productive. Our workloads tend to increase as we absorb the work of employees who retire or leave and are not replaced. It's likely that your job requirements are changing rapidly. Common requirements are professional education and maintaining certifications. You focus on improving yourself to improve your job security. One thing is certain: for most of us, work can be all-consuming.

The good news is that many HR departments around the country are recognizing the impact of caregiving on their employees. Many are offering flextime (often extended to new mothers) to those caring for older parents. A friend of mine who was working for a large East Coast firm was able to take a six-month leave of absence to help her mother through cancer treatments. Bon Secours Hospital (Virginia) could well serve as a model for other employers. In fact, you could suggest some of these options to your employer. Bon Secours offers its employees ten days a year of emergency in-home care at a 50 percent reduced rate, respite services, discounts on long-term care, and a Grandpartners Program that invites older people to volunteer at the onsite child care center.[8]

Despite the costs to employers for such programs, businesses will have to find ways to accommodate workers who are caregivers. Otherwise, they will face the reality of higher employee absenteeism, increased health problems, and quite possibly the cost of replacing a worker who feels they have no choice but to leave. According to the recent MetLife Study of Working Caregivers and Employer Health Care Costs[9], employees caring for an older relative are more likely to have depression, diabetes, hypertension, or heart disease, costing employers an estimated additional health care cost of 8 percent per year, or $13.4 billion annually.

Before you think, "I can handle it. I can balance both my job and caregiving responsibilities," note these conclusions from a survey commissioned by the National Alliance for Caregiving. Two-thirds of those caregivers surveyed reported late to work or took time off during the workday because of caregiving issues. For one out of five surveyed, demands were so great that they had to take a leave of absence. Ten percent felt they had to rearrange their work schedule or change to a less demanding job.[10]

Family Responsibilities

Of course, you must also consider the responsibilities you have to your own immediate family. Several years ago, I had an excellent employee who faced caring for her mother through a five-year battle with cancer. She would work 7 AM to 4 PM each day. After work, she immediately went to her mother's house to prepare dinner and do the evening care for her mother, then head home to cook for her family and care for her two teenagers. I finally convinced her to utilize the Family Medical Leave Act (FMLA) and take time off. Throughout her ordeal, she often remarked it was her family who really suffered (and herself, of course).

Newly married couples are told that their commitment is now to their spouse. Well, this is the time your commitment should be to *your* family. Don't think you can give 100 percent to your parent, 100 percent to your job, and still have the time and energy to give to your own family. It is impossible in the long run.

There is a very powerful video I shared with my subscribers at TransitionAgingParents.com awhile back. A young family decides to move across country to care for an aging parent. In the video, the family reflects on the changing and unexpected demands of caring for their aging father/grandfather. "At 83, Herbie suffers from dementia and can no longer live alone. (The family) is faced with difficult choices and overwhelming responsibility as they charge head on through their Sandwich years. It is a story of love, family dynamics and the immeasurable sacrifice of those who are caught in the middle."11 http://vimeo.com/1340561

Support Network

Consider your support network *now*. Think about each category below. A good idea is to make a list of names of people you can call on for help. If you've lost touch, write a note, send an email, or make a phone call. Making time for a quick face-to-face meeting will yield renewed connection and support, and could also offer other ideas of support.

Personal friends. If your friends are local, it is well worth connecting in person, perhaps over a cup of coffee. Catch up on their lives and share how your life is changing. They may very well have another person or resource that will turn out to be most helpful to you.

If your friends are long-distance friends, they can still be a tremendous support to you. My childhood friend and I, although living six hundred miles apart, have stayed in touch over the years, at first by mail, then email. She was the first person I called upon learning of my mother's hospitalization and possible stroke. She worked for an area hospital and was a great help in finding resources and answers to my questions. Because of our deep relationship, she also offered to be there for me when I needed her. I would often call her at midnight to unload my frustrations and sometimes cry on her shoulder. Each of us needs a friend like this. I trusted her completely, and she supported me completely.

So, what if you've lost touch over the years and don't know how to reconnect? A simple note, phone call, or email, or friending on Facebook can open up that line of communication. Start out by building that relationship; just don't start unloading on a person from out of the blue. They will be less likely to want to make the connection.

Colleagues at work. We all have personal friends at work. These people often become like our second families. Here's a word of caution about how much you share about your personal life with casual friends or supervisors at work. This may backfire. That same excellent employee (now with another firm) told me she no longer can share anything about her personal life because if there is a problem, her supervisor automatically says out loud, "Well, that's because she is dealing with this or that family problem." There is good reason to keep your personal life and concerns out of your business environment. If you need to make different work arrangements due to caregiving demands, I advise first checking with your HR department to understand your options, and have them advise you on how best to proceed with your supervisor.

Employer support. Your company may have various policies that you can utilize. These policies may include flex scheduling, telecommuting, or job sharing. I mentioned the FMLA earlier. You should familiarize yourself with your rights under this and any additional state laws that allow for job protections while taking care of an ill family member. Your HR department can direct you to the appropriate information or agencies. Also, if your company has an Employee Assistance Program (EAP), it's an excellent way for you to share your situation with an objective third party who understands you and your company. EAP services include assessment, support and referrals.

Your place of worship and your parent's place of worship. Reach out to members, visitation and support groups, and nonaffiliated groups that may use the facilities. Cultivate a relationship with the pastoral and office staff.

Organizations you belong to. If you belong to any community organizations, PTA, boards of nonprofits, or service organizations, you likely have friendships and support you can draw upon.

Stop! Time for a Sanity Check.

What are your priorities? It seems we go through life adding more and more activities and commitments. Now is the time to reflect on the priorities in your life. What is important to you and what is not? How will you establish a *new* balance in your life?

Also, make it a part of your daily life to think about each and every interaction you have. Can this person be a possible support person or perhaps suggest another person or resource to you? Know that most people want to help others if they know the need. Don't leave any stone unturned in building your support network.

Chapter 4

Discuss ... As A Family: *Create Your Plan*

K now that you are not alone! You cannot do this alone. You will not survive with your health and mental state intact. And your parent will miss out on what the rest of her family has to offer.

But "discuss and decide as a family?" You may be thinking, "No way. My siblings and I have opposite perspectives, lifestyles, priorities, etc." For just a moment, think about yourself and your dreams for your own children. One of the hopes for my own children (as I raised them) was that they would have mutual respect for each other, grow up to be friends, and remain close. I didn't have that with my brother growing up. But I realized it would mean the world to my mother to have my brother and me working together in her best interest. It was not easy for me. It was certainly not natural. And there were times when I had to step away from a conversation with him so I would not say things I regretted. But I always kept in mind "we both want what's best for our mother."

Put yourself in your parent's shoes. How do you think your elderly parent feels when she/he sees the family arguing, split over issues? It probably upsets and stresses them. They are likely thinking, "And this is the legacy I'm leaving the world!" Working together with our siblings is one of the best gifts we can give our parents. A *goal of peaceful co-existence* is something we should strive for.

The Scope.

Determine the scope of the transition. *Scope* **is what the transition includes and what it does not include.**

Regardless of what change you are dealing with, take time to reflect on the scope of the change. Defining scope is about defining your desired outcome. I'm reminded of Stephen Covey saying, "If the ladder is not leaning against the right wall, every step we take just gets us to the wrong place faster."

You may think something like taking the car keys to stop your parent from driving is one action: take the keys away. But as part of that decision, you'll also have to find alternative modes of transportation for your parent, and you'll want to cancel their auto insurance. There's the whole issue of what to do with the car. Perhaps your parent would find meaning in donating her car to charity or selling it to someone in need.

Once you determine what is included in the change, you'll need to define what is "out of bounds" for this particular change. Just keep the focus on transportation-related issues. You would not get into the discussion of selling your parent's home and moving them to assisted living just because they could no longer drive. Avoid out of bounds items. Keep the issue and discussion focused.

It would be nice if all challenges could easily and clearly be defined to one action. But more often than not, we will be immersed in an urgent, frenzied situation when our aging parent has a major health or life crisis. For months or years prior to the event, you'll experience some level of anxiety about your aging parent, their challenges, and decline. But often it takes a crisis to bring a family to action. It can be so overwhelming that you don't know where to start. It happens to just about every family. In his book, *My Mother, Your Mother: Embracing "Slow_Medicine,"* geriatrician Dennis McCullough describes crisis as one of the stages of aging. So when it happens, accept it as another challenge for you and your family to work through. McCullough says to let go of the "why's and what if's" and focus on "what now."

When confronted with multiple, complex problems, your challenge is indeed great. But if you break the situation into steps and prioritize, you will help your parent, and along the way, probably strengthen your relationship.

So here is the formula to determine scope of the transition (change):

- Define the end goal or outcome.
- Break the work required into manageable pieces (tasks).
- Set boundaries for what you will not deal with.

Another example, using the formula:

1. Mother wishes to age-in-place after a health crisis.
2. Manageable pieces may include obtaining an evaluation for aging-in-place, a personal emergency response system (PERS), a home care aide, a cleaning service, or Meals on Wheels.
3. Out of bounds: discussion to sell her car, visits to senior living facilities.

The Participants

It's important to have your parent be centrally involved. However, if your parent is very ill or has dementia, she may not be able to attend, but should still be kept in the loop about options and agreement. You'll want to keep the number of participants small and manageable. Be sure to include siblings and anyone integral to your parent's care (such as a parent's sibling, home care aide or trusted advisor). Family members who are needed but cannot attend due to distance should be encouraged to Skype or conference call in.

Pre-Planning

Pre-Planning for the family meeting is so important. You started doing this in Step 1. You began to share information with the rest of your family members, helping them to warm up to the situation at hand. Continue to listen to their insights, concerns, and conflicts of interest. You don't have to agree or disagree at this point. Active listening is probably the best thing you can do right now. Have you ever noticed how people often answer their own questions just by verbalizing their thoughts and feelings? Letting that happen facilitates each person meeting the change and challenge in their own way.

The Family Meeting

Here are the essential items in a family meeting:
   In advance:

- Decide who the facilitator is. Depending on the type of issue you are dealing with, options include a geriatric care manager or a social worker. If you're dealing with a financial or legal issue, you could ask a financial advisor or attorney to facilitate. You may want to seek out an Eldercare Mediator (a new type of professional) who can smooth this transition without being involved for the long haul.
- Put suggested topics into an agenda.
- Prioritize issues and set a time limit for each issue and the overall meeting.

- Prepare a summary of the assessment you've done.
- Prepare a list of suggested guidelines for the meeting.

At the meeting:

- Reach consensus on guidelines for the meeting (such as when someone is speaking, others cannot interrupt).
- Discuss the issue(s) that your parent is facing. If your parent is present, make sure her voice is heard. If not present, keep her needs as the priority.
- Determine what needs to be done—The Plan (see below).
- Divide up the duties. Allow people to volunteer. This will help people feel they have a choice to draw upon their strengths. It will also help them feel respected and acknowledged.

You may doubt the ability of your family to get through a family meeting. You may be thinking something like this. "Our family will not even be able to get past the first item on the agenda. My sister will start talking and never stop. My brother will jump from issue to issue. And I will get so upset I'll want to leave the room."

I suggest you share a book with each family member involved before the meeting. It's *Crucial Conversations: Tools for Talking When the Stakes are High*, by Kerry Patterson. You'll read about tools to handle difficult situations and important conversations, such as those at a family meeting. Patterson provides wonderful instruction on how to create the right conditions for dialogue, using his STATE method:

- Share your facts
- Tell your story
- Ask for others' paths
- Talk tentatively
- Encourage testing

The Plan

This is a critical and vital piece. You cannot leave the family meeting without a plan. It should be well-defined enough that each person involved understands decisions made and each person's commitments. Someone can set up a simple spreadsheet to include all this information. Date the plan and give each person a copy. Get a copy out to each attendee as soon as possible after the family meeting. You may also need to schedule another family meeting to share any follow-up research, and to be sure everyone is on the same page right before the transition. It all depends on how simple or complex the transition is.

The Plan needs to include:

- *Task*—What needs to be accomplished.
- *Owner*—Who needs to do it.
- *Completion date*—When it needs to be done.
- *Purpose*—Why it's being done.
- *Go-to person*—If problems or obstacles arise, the responsible person to reach out to for help.
- *Follow-up*—How and when the responsible party communicates back to the whole group.

Here is a simple Excel template for your plan. Adjust as needed.

Task	Owner	Completion Date	Purpose	Go-to Person	Follow-up / When & How

Do not strive for perfection. If you've got a perfectionist in the group, emphasize the importance of moving ahead to best help your aging parent. I love the phrase, *better done than perfect.*

Consensus

Before you walk away from the family meeting, everyone should be in consensus. Not everyone will agree 100 percent with everything decided, but they can decide if they can *live with the decision.* Always keep in mind the best interest of your parent. You will be balancing cost with benefits. Some may be shocked by the price of services that you may be seeking. Don't let cost be an initial barrier to some service or product. There are many sources of financial assistance for the elderly (outlined later in Step 4, Resources.). Seek the right service or product, and then you can seek out aid or negotiate for a lower price.

The Plan's Impact on You and Your Immediate Family

Now turn to yourself, your family, and your other responsibilities. Think about how you can integrate this additional work into your schedule. If you think you can add it on top of an already over-loaded schedule, think again. Consider what outside activities you can perhaps drop temporarily. (For example, if you serve as an officer on a board, consider temporarily dropping the officer position or dropping the board position, while still being a volunteer.)

Talk with your spouse and children about the family meeting and what it will mean specifically to you: your new time commitments, concerns, and anxieties. Ask for their emotional support as well as their support in helping with things at home. Perhaps your spouse can do some Internet research or phone calls to investigate possible resources and options. Depending on the age of your children, they can take on some tasks as well. Even young children can make get-well cards for Grandma.

Benefits of the Plan

The very act of creating the plan brings the family together to reach consensus and commitment. The process opens up lines of communication, draws upon the strength of each family member, and builds trust.

A key benefit is that the plan gets the entire family on the same page. The very nature of a plan sets up accountability by those who have worked to create it. It is the roadmap for what needs to be done for your aging parent.

Stop! Time for a Sanity Check.

This was a huge topic. Do you see how a family meeting, although possibly scary to think of, can be so very helpful for your aging parent and family? The first time you go through this process, it will likely feel awkward, and you may get resistance from family members. Pay close attention to the pre-meeting steps, selection of an impartial, knowledgeable facilitator, and follow-up to all the tasks in the detailed plan.

Chapter 5

Plan: *Seek and You Will Find*

When you're facing a crisis or even "just" an issue with an aging parent, it is hard to know where to begin the search. There are so many Web sites and books out there. I am going to share my key resources with you. These are the basic references I turn to first, regardless of the problem.

My first two "go to" resources are:

1. The book *How to Care for Aging Parents* by Virginia Morris. This book stays out on my desk and is the first place I turn to for information. It is a one-stop resource for all the medical, financial, housing, emotional, and practical issues you may face. The author is an authority on eldercare, was caregiver for her two parents, and writes in an empathetic, easy-to-understand style. The appendices of resources are excellent.

2. The Web site Eldercare Locator (http://www.eldercare .gov). This site is maintained by the U.S. Administration on Aging. By putting in a zip code or city name, you can obtain the contact information for any Area Agency on Aging. This is a starting point to find trusted senior

services in any part of the country. The site also offers excellent fact sheets about a variety of topics.

Informational Associations

If your parent is dealing with a specific health problem, I strongly advise you to check out the related association Web sites. There you will find trusted information about the condition/disease, have access to recent research, and be a better advocate and caregiver for your parent.

1. *Alzheimer's Association.* http://www.alz.org This is a phenomenal site, providing information and referrals to local chapters that will lead you to local services and support groups. This association also serves those with other forms of dementia. Even if you or your parent do not need the services of this organization, it is likely that some friend or other family member will.

2. Two of the common chronic health conditions of the elderly are diabetes and cardiovascular disease (including stroke). Below are their association Web sites, providing information, helpful living tips, and referrals to local doctors and support groups.

   a. *American Diabetes Association.* http://www.diabetes.org/

   b. *American Heart Association.* http://www.americanheart.org

3. If your parent has another disease or disorder, just Google it, seeking out its official association Web site.

Two more very important Web sites for any elderly person are:

1. Benefits Checkup. http://benefitscheckup.org/ Developed and maintained by The National Council on Aging

(NCOA), it connects seniors with 1,800 public and private benefits programs from all 50 states and D.C. Their site states, *"As of Saturday, February 6, 2010, we have helped 2,431,193 people find over $8 billion worth of annual benefits they deserve."*

2. Centers for Medicare & Medicaid Services, http://mymedicare.gov/ One of its key features is a robust comparison tool for health/drug plans based on plan availability in your geographic area, your specific health and prescription drug needs, and quality and cost. I give this tool an A+ and use it annually to help my mother make her Medicare D choice during Open Enrollment each year (Nov 15-Dec 31).

Experts

Depending on what issue you are addressing, here is a list of possible expertise you are looking for and the related professional organization that provides certification in that area.

1. *Aging in Place.* CAPS (Certified Aging in Place). Learn what this certification can mean to you as you seek expertise in your location. Find CAPS individuals and businesses by your zip code. http://www.nahb.org/page.aspx/category/sectionID=686

2. *Geriatric Care Manager.* Find out what the various levels of certification mean as you seek expertise. Find certified care managers by your zip code. http://www.caremanager.org/displaycommon.cfm?an=1&subarticlenbr=94

3. *Eldercare Law.* Find out what an Elder Law attorney can do for you. Find an elder law attorney in your area. http://www.naela.org/

4. *Elder Finances.* www.napfa.org The National Association of Personal Financial Advisors provides a list of fee-based

financial planners who can assist with personal finances and estate planning.

Financial Assistance

Here is a list of possible funding sources for your parent.

1. Ask potential providers if there are any *current or anticipated discounts*. This is the easiest and fastest way to save on costs. I did this with my mother's prospective retirement community and received a $10k savings on her entrance fee. And, after my mother asked, her physician switched her to almost all generic drugs for a hefty cost savings.

2. Benefits CheckUp was mentioned above, but warrants mentioning again. This site helps those aged fifty-five and older find federal, state, and local benefit programs as well as prescription drug programs for which they are eligible.

3. Veterans Aid and Attendance Benefit. This is a "pension benefit" and not dependent upon service-related injuries. Aid and Attendance can help pay for care in the home, nursing home, or assisted living. A veteran is eligible for up to $1,632 per month, while a surviving spouse is eligible for $1,055 per month. A couple is eligible for up to $1,949 per month. For more information, visit http://www.veteranaid.org/

4. Senior Living Line of Credit. This is very similar in nature to the Home Equity Line of Credit that my mother used. But the "Senior Living" line is different in that it is typically unsecured, and enables up to six persons to apply together (so the burden is shared among siblings). Loan documents specify that this is for a parent's housing and care. This is a good option if your parent wants to move into a senior living community but can't sell their

home immediately. http://www.elderlifefinancial.com/access/assisted_living_loan_home.aspx

5. Last but not least, your Area Agency on Aging is an excellent resource for items such as home heating assistance, low cost transportation options, and more. In my personal experience, they researched my question (at no cost) and got back to me in a timely manner. http://www.eldercare.gov

Support Resources for Caregivers

1. http://www.caring.com/ Information and resources for families of elderly loved ones.
2. www.caregiving.com Information and support resources for caregivers.
3. www.caps4caregivers.org Resources for children of aging parents.
4. www.caregiver.org Family Caregiver Alliance.
5. www.caregiver911.com Caregiver Survival Resources.

Consider both face-to-face support groups and online groups. There are pros and cons to each format. The face-to-face groups provide a sense of belonging which can be helpful in dealing with the isolation in your day-to-day caregiving. You can be with other people who can understand and empathize with your experiences and emotions, and even share tips and coping strategies. A word of caution: sometimes these face-to-face groups can be dominated by one person griping and overtaking all discussion. It's easier to disregard someone like this in an online group. You just ignore their postings. Also, the online groups provide a certain sense of anonymity. You can post any time of the day. Sometimes just the act of posting, allowing you to vent, can make you feel better. Also, most of the online groups offer a facilitator who will offer suggestions and guidance.

Stop! Time for a Sanity Check.

Take some time now to check out local and online resources. As you can tell by my list above, there is a lot to investigate based on your parent's particular needs and the type of transition she/he is facing. Share this load of work with other family members. Then when you all reconvene, either by phone or at an in-person meeting, you can share all you've learned and decide which resources your family will utilize.

Some of you may be comfortable with in-person support groups, and some may prefer an online group. It's really great that so many options exist. Pick the ones that are right for you and focus on those.

Chapter 6

Transition: *Carry Out the Plan.*

Before the transition—One last check

When you reach this stage, you have done many major steps and the really important relationship building. You have decided what the actual change will be, reached a consensus with your parent and family, and drafted a plan (who will do what, when, why, and how). Different members of your family have accepted responsibility for different parts of the transition. You have done your research and found trusted resources to guide the transition and possibly help mediate any sticky points with your family.

If you still feel anxious and stressed, know that those feelings are completely natural. It's just not your aging parent who is going through a change. This change will impact each and every member of the family, including you. You've got to get through the change and find the new status quo—until next time! And that is the nature of our world and of aging. As I helped my mother transition, I found myself thinking about my own elderly years and how my children and I would interact. You will likely feel intense emotions, some of which you can identify, others that you cannot.

Right before the transition, it's a good idea to update the spreadsheet identifying everyone's assigned roles and tasks, and send it to all involved family members.

Follow-up Family Meeting

Review the plan. Ensure everyone has done what they promised, and are available for the actual transition/process.

Make the transition

This is where all your hard work begins to pay off.

- Allow enough time so your aging parent is not rushed.
- Have one person assigned to Mom to answer questions, concerns, and address any perceived problems as soon as possible. Remember, perception is reality.
- Think proactively. If you see an opportunity to help Mom adjust, step up and ask. The day my mother moved into her retirement community, I realized she knew nobody to go to breakfast with her first morning. I asked the director if they had a buddy system. They said they could indeed match Mom up with a buddy to show her the ropes.
- If more than one family member has tasks to do, pick a time for a meet-up or call-in so everyone can report.
- The key is to have everyone feel this is going smoothly. Reduce the chaos, the anxiety, and the stress. You do that with the plan you created. You may certainly have to adjust the plan. That is to be expected and is something you can deal with.
- At the end of the transition (whether it's having home modifications done, moving to assisted living, taking the car keys away), do something positive. Enjoy a meal together. Order carryout to make it easy and fun. The

point here is to celebrate that, regardless of the transition, you are all still the same family. And you have all worked together to make the change.

Review—Lessons Learned

A week after the transition

- Reflect about the recent transition. In your mind, consider what went well and what didn't.
- In an informal conversation with your parent, ask what in her mind went well and what didn't. Keep the conversation open-ended. Ask and then just listen. You don't have to interject a lot of your own perspective. This way, you'll gain a better insight into how to better prepare for the next transition you will face together.
- Ask each family member who was involved to share what went well and what didn't. This feedback will help the next transition!

Stop! Time for a Sanity Check

By the end of my mother's transition (moving out of her home and into a retirement community), I was incredibly dirty, tired, and exhausted, both physically and emotionally. Be kind to yourself. Give yourself time and a place to recover. It will not be unusual to get complaints as part of the feedback you'll receive. As I've said throughout this book, be patient and flexible, and stay focused on what is best for your parent. None of this is easy. But each transition is an opportunity to meet the needs of your aging parent and help your bond grow stronger.

Chapter 7

Post-Transition: *Leave the Past Behind. Embrace the Future. You Are on This Walk Together!*

A fter the change or transition has taken place, know that it may take your parent (and the family) time to adjust. When my mother moved into her retirement community, although she had been 100 percent ready to move in, the reality of the move was quite disturbing to her. An otherwise calm, quiet woman, her temper flared suddenly. I will admit I did not handle it very well. But we have to accept our failings and move on. I kept reminding myself that I was human, and I would try harder next time. Photos of my mother taken that day show a very unhappy woman. We all just backed off, carried out our plan, and tried to be supportive of each other and respectful of Mom's feelings. I recall it taking all the energy and patience I could muster.

Feedback From Others

Keep everyone in the loop and be receptive to feedback

In many of today's families, it is unusual for all the siblings and family members to live locally to the aging parent. It is also necessary for someone to step forward to be the "primary" caregiver. Even though I live six hundred miles from my mother, I am considered to be her primary caregiver. I know firsthand that even though I felt enormous stress and anxiety when my mother was in crisis, it would have been far easier and faster for me to make decisions alone than to work with my brother. But that certainly was not in my mother's best interest, in the long term.

Siblings and family members who are not included in decision making will likely feel left out, anxious, and helpless about their parent's situation. Don't leave them out! Non-primary caregivers have the benefit of time and/or distance and can identify important changes in your parent. They can also offer respite to the primary caregiver. Everyone has something to offer. The bottom line is we need to be inclusive and accepting of all who are integral to the care of an aging parent.

Visits

Schedule regular visits and/or phone calls. Visit and call when you say you will. The elderly look forward to these. Don't underestimate their importance. When spending time with your parent, let them lead the conversation. Ask how their friends are. It's just another way to set the tone of mutuality.

We all fall into a slump occasionally. For my mother, she finds it hard to return to normal life after vacation and visiting my brother or me. I liken it to the let-down that's so common after Christmas.

I was talking with a good friend about how to help our parents with this. She said, "Choose happiness—why not?" What a great thought. We wake up each day and even though we struggle with aches, pains and worries, we can choose how we will face life that day. So while I listen to my mom and validate her feelings, I'll also gently turn the conversation and inquire about the good things happening in her life. I ask her, "Mom, what are you happy about?" Before she knows it, she's confirming the stuff that makes her happy. You know how they say, if you smile, you'll feel better. When Mom chats about what makes her happy, I actually hear her voice change.

Holidays

While everyone has family traditions for the holidays, let your parent take the lead in how they want to celebrate the holidays. In our family, my mother would fly to my home for Thanksgiving and then travel to my brother's for Christmas. The sometimes nasty blizzard or illnesses at gatherings caused my mother to decide to stay at her retirement community for Christmas and New Year's. Last year was her first year to be away from family. I felt incredibly guilty and almost drove the six hundred miles so she would not be alone. But we ended up calling as a family and chatting, and she had dinner with her close friends. We opened our gifts as we talked on the phone.

It really is your parent's decision to make. Old family traditions end. New traditions emerge.

Vacations

Summer is a great time for travel with your aging parent, if they are able. It will lift their spirits, create new shared memories for both of you, and give them something special to look forward to. It takes some planning to ensure we consider their special needs (decreased mobility, dietary needs, and easier fatigue). At one point my mother told me she didn't think she'd ever fly again.

But then last summer she said yes to an offer to visit us. I came up with some ways to make the trip easier for her.

I found her a nonstop flight to minimize any air travel hassles. It just meant I drove two hours into Chicago to meet her at the gate. She asked for a wheelchair at check-in that took her through a special security area and meant much less waiting. We planned her flight for early afternoon to avoid traffic at either end of her trip. The planning really paid off.

While here, we made short outings to the library, to a beach with nearby parking, and a trip into Chicago to sit by the lake and have dinner with my son. She seems to enjoy meeting people and seeing new places, so I used that as a guide for our activities.

One thing I found important was to find out how she felt each day of her visit, share the list of options, listen to what she'd like to do, and then be flexible.

Your Parent's Legacy

Every time I'm with my mother, I hear a new story about her childhood. And I keep thinking I've got to capture all these and get them down into her "life story." She does not like to write, but I sure do. So there's nothing to stop me.

David Solie, in his book, *How to Say It to Seniors: Closing the Communication_Gap with Our Elders*, tells us that there are two major factors driving the elderly. One is the drive to control their life. The other is the drive to define their legacy. Yes, even in this later stage of life that many see as a period of decline, our parents are moving forward in a new psychological developmental phase. They are working to make sense of their life and leave behind their legacy.

Even before I met David and read his book, I discovered an elderly friend writing her legacy. When she handed me her book, I remarked how pretty the cover was and then realized she was the author! It had taken her ten years to write, but she had her life history recorded in a published biography. She was so proud, and she had included wonderful pictures, poems, and stories. I felt as if I held a treasure in my hands.

So how can we help our aging parents write their life story? Are there techniques to trigger memories and their details and make that life story as rich as possible?

Here are five ideas I came up with:

1. Use Google Earth to locate the places your parent has lived. Check out any photos and the surrounding streets. My mom and I did this on her last visit. She was amazed with the technology, and the street names triggered lots of childhood memories that she shared. It was great fun.
2. Take your parent back to their birthplace. My mother and I did this not too long ago. We found where her old one-room schoolhouse had been, the farm her parents rented and cared for, and the gravesites of her grandparents. We found ourselves talking into the wee hours of the morning during that trip.
3. Purchase a digital photo frame. I plan to scan in many of my mother's old pictures, load them into the digital frame, and give it to her as a gift. I know this will mean a lot to her, and will be another way for us to talk about her memories.
4. Have younger members of the family, perhaps grandchildren, "interview" your parent on video or audio cassette. They can ask what life was like when they were young, who their friends were, and what they enjoyed doing. I recall when I was young I couldn't visualize my grandparents as children until they started telling their stories. I have a vivid memory of my grandmother describing the fear she felt every morning running down the farm lane to school past a bull that was only separated from her by a fence.
5. Consider Bcelebrated.com's product/service that provides a process to capture your parent's autobiography. (See Appendix A.)

Where Do You Go from Here?

As I bring this book to an end, I find myself thinking about the many daughters and sons who have shared their stories with me. They embody stories of love and respect for their parents, of courage, perseverance, and often sacrifice. There is Mary, who struggles as a long-distance caregiver from one thousand miles away trying to help her two elderly parents with declining health. There is Paul, who is helping his elderly father face the end of his life, recognizing a life well-lived and making the most of each day. And there is Robbie, who has managed to balance the end of her corporate career while caring for her mother with cancer.

They have opened my eyes to one certainty. Each of us is unique, as are our parents and their situations. None of us can foresee the future. But we can be prepared. I hope that my ADAPT® framework will be one of your tools. Remember "Assess, Discuss As a family, Plan, and Transition" as you guide your parent through their many transitions.

I leave you with a wonderful quote by Mother Teresa: "Do small things with great love." This framework will put the structure in place so you can truly focus on the "small things" for your parent.

Appendix A:

Three Awesome Products/Services

Bcelebrated

http://www.bcelebrated.com/

Bcelebrated is one of the most uplifting and well-designed services I have encountered. You can capture your (or your aging parent's) autobiography and email addresses of your family/friends and also store password-protected letters to loved ones. In the event of your death, the administrators you assign will turn your site into a memorial and trigger emails to be sent to all of your contacts. It is a user-friendly service that can mean so much to you and your family.

Virtual Dementia Tour Kit

(http://secondwind.org/)

I immersed myself for fifteen minutes in using the "Virtual Dementia Tour" kit. It totally changed my perception of dementia. In fact, I can't get the experience out of my mind. Let me share my experience with you.

What's in the kit?

- *An information booklet.*
- *Goggles* simulating macular degeneration.
- *Gloves* simulating arthritis and diminished motor skills.
- *Vinyl shoe inserts* simulating neuropathy which caused my feet to hurt the whole time, standing or walking.
- *The CD for the virtual tour*, emulating the hearing of those with dementia. It is well-designed and most effective!

What is the process?

I found my portable CD player and headphones and asked my husband to stand by in case I started to fall. He said it was strange to watch me talking to myself as I "entered the confusion state."

I started the CD and took the "Before" test of several questions, rating how I felt about myself and also my perception of someone with dementia. Then I put on the goggles and gloves and inserted the shoe pieces.

As the Dementia Tour began, I heard a cacophony of sounds that made it almost impossible to hear the instructions. I had trouble remembering the simple, consecutive instructions and didn't do any of the tasks very well! Occasionally there would be a very loud siren and other disruptive sounds. The tour seemed a lot longer than fifteen minutes.

It was such a relief when the tour ended, the noise stopped, and I was able to take out the inserts. I realized I was feeling tired, off-balance, and disoriented.

What did I learn?

I found that:

- It takes a lot of time to do a simple task and why we need to give simple requests, one at a time.

- Being bombarded with noise and stimuli is tiring and frustrating.
- My reality (in the simulation) was far different from a normal person's.
- Every one of my senses was impacted.

Who could benefit from using this Individual/Family Virtual Dementia Tour kit?

- Family members of someone with dementia.
- Adult children with aging parents.
- Caregivers for the aged.

I can honestly say there is no article, no book, no checklist, or no instructional course that would prepare me like this experience did. I now understand why it's so important to give those with dementia extra time, lots of patience and calm, and a positive and loving attitude. Meet them where they are!

Would I recommend it to others? Absolutely!

Famililink

(http://famililink.com/)

Famililink enabled my mother to send her first email, ever! Last summer, while visiting us, my mother logged on to a computer for the first time in her life, sent an email, received photos from me, and set up her calendar, all in one portal.

I'm convinced the only way I got her online was Famililink's one-stop portal. CEO Laura Nuhann states that "Famililink is unique compared to other Web sites and software offerings that focus primarily on caregiving resources and support, whereas Famililink's purpose is to improve the communication between the family and their aging loved ones while making it possible to engage the care recipient in the process."

What are the key features that make this product a good choice for your elderly parent?

First and foremost, the visual design, colors used, and size of font are excellent. This immediately appealed to my mother.

Once Mom logged in, her front page showed photos, her daily calendar, and large colorful buttons for easy navigation to Mail, Pictures, Contacts, and Calendar. My mom loved it that when I sent her an email with photos attached, those photos automatically appeared on her front page.

There is a prominent button on Mom's front page, "Send Urgent Message." If she has an emergency, she clicks this button and a pre-formatted emergency email message appears. She clicks "Send," and I immediately receive it.

My mother was able to add me as a "helper" so I can log in and answer her questions. In my opinion, this is a key feature that helped my mother get past the initial learning curve.

We found this software easy to learn, easy to use, and well-supported. A big part of getting your parent to use software (especially someone who has never touched a computer) is to walk them through it step by step. I was surprised my mother didn't even know where the letters were on the keyboard. It was slow going, but we sat together, and finally Mom sent and received her first email, viewed her photos, and updated her calendar. I said, "Mom, you have now entered the digital age." You should have seen the smile on her face.

Appendix B:

Resources

Alzheimer's Association: alz.org or 800.272.3900 80000. 272.3900

American Diabetes Association: www.diabetes.org or 800. Diabetes

American Heart Association: www.americanheart.org or 800.242 .8721

A Place For Mom: http://www.aplaceformom.com/ (free referral service for home care, senior living, and other senior options)

Benefits Checkup: www.benefitscheckup.org

Children of Aging Parents: www.caps4caregivers.org (information/referrals)

Centers for Medicare & Medicaid: http://www.cms.hhs.gov/ or 800.Medicare

Crucial Conversations: Tools for Talking When Stakes are High by Kerry Patterson (New York: McGraw-Hill, 2002)

Eldercare Locator (referral to your local Area Agency on Aging): www.eldercare.gov or 800.677.1116

"Home Safety: How Well Does Your Home Meet Your Needs?" (Checklist) http://assets.aarp.org/external_sites/caregiving /checklists/checklist_homeSafety.html

How to Care for Aging Parents by Virginia Morris (New York: Workman, 2004)

How to Say it to Seniors: Closing the Communication Gap with our Elders by David Solie (New York: Prentice Hall, 2004)

My Mother, Your Mother: Embracing Slow Medicine by Dennis McCullough (New York: HarperCollins, 2009)

National Association of Home Builders (to find a CAPS certified builder or remodeler by city/zip code): http://www.nahb .org/directory.aspx?sectionID=717&directoryID=387

National Association of Geriatric Care Managers. http://www .caremanager.org/ or 520.881.8008

National Association of Elder Law. http://www.naela.org/ or 703-942-5711

National Association of Personal Financial Advisors. http://www .napfa.org/ or 847-483-5400

Veterans Aid and Attendance Benefit (information for getting started): http://www.veteranaid.org/program.php

About the Author

D ale C. Carter holds an MBA from Indiana University. Formerly an educator and project manager, Dale is now an advocate for our elderly by reaching out to their adult children. In 2009, she founded Transition Aging Parents (TransitionAgingParents.com). In providing relevant information and insight to adult children, she enables them to help their aging parents "thrive and find joy in every stage of life." Through her radio show, e-courses, articles, and presentations, Dale helps family caregivers navigate the challenges of caregiving, as well as find purpose and fulfillment in what is truly some of the most important work of their lives.

END NOTES

1. *National Alliance for Caregiving and AARP, Caregiving in the U.S., 2009* http://www.aarp.org/aarp/presscenter/pressrelease/articles/caregiving_survey_release.html

2. *How to Care for Aging Parents*, Virginia Morris,p.284.

3. "Time Flies." TorontoSun.com, November 29, 2009. http://www.torontosun.com/life/healthandfitness/2009/11/25/119 25281.html

4. Centers for Disease Control and Prevention. http://www.cdc.gov/HomeandRecreationalSafety/falls/adultfalls.html

5. Home Instead Senior Care. "40-70 rule." http://www.homeinstead.com/resource/4070/default.aspx

6. "Life Expectancy in US Hits New High." Health Day, December 16, 2009. http://www.nlm.nih.gov/medlineplus/news/fullstory_93077.html

7. ""2008 Progress Report on Alzheimer's Disease: Moving Forward." National Institute on Aging. http://www.nia.nih.gov/Alzheimers/Publications/ADProgress2008/

8. "Demands Grown on Workers Who are Caregivers at Home." AARP Bulletin Today, December 8, 2009. http://bulletin.aarp .org/yourworld/family/articles/demands_grow_on_workers_who _are_caregivers_at_home.html

9. MetLife Mature Market Institute, "The MetLife Study of Working Caregivers and Employer Health Care Costs," February 2010. http://www.metlife.com/assets/cao/mmi/publications/ studies/2010/mmi-working-caregivers-employers-health-care-costs.pdf

10. National Alliance for Caregiving. "Caregiving in the U.S. 2009, A Focused Look at Those Caring for Someone Age 50 or Older." http://www.caregiving.org/data/CaregivingUSAllAges ExecSum.pdf

11. *The   Sandwich   Generation*—The   Trailer.   http:// vimeo.com/1340561